Note to Parents and Teachers

The READING ABOUT: STARTERS series introduces key science vocabulary to young children while encouraging them to discover and understand the world around them. The series works as a set of graded readers in three levels.

LEVEL 2: BEGIN TO READ ALONE follows guidelines set out in the National Curriculum for Year 2 in schools. These books can be read alone or as part of guided or group reading. Each book has three sections:

• Information pages that introduce key words. These key words appear in bold for easy recognition on pages where the related science concepts are explained.
• A lively story that recalls this vocabulary and encourages children to use these words when they talk and write.
• A quiz and index ask children to look back and recall what they have read.

Questions for Further Investigation

WHAT TIME IS IT? explains key concepts about TIME. Here are some suggestions for further discussion linked to the questions on the information spreads:

p. 5 *When do we need to know what time it is?* Encourage children to think of everyday examples, e.g. school hours, opening hours for shops, timetables for trains and buses, TV viewing guides. Point out that people such as farmers and fishermen depend on natural timetables, e.g. seasons, daylight hours, high and low tides.

7 *How long do you take to brush your teeth each night?* e.g. A couple of minutes. Ask children about other activities that usually take seconds, minutes or hours.

p. 9 *Will the small bowl sink slower than the big silver bowl?* No, it sinks faster (if the hole is the same size). Because the bowl should always take the same amount of time to sink, e.g. 1 minute, it can be used to time activities that take 1 minute, like an eggtimer.

p. 11 *What sounds tell us the time?* Church bells tell us the hour, as do chiming clocks and cuckoo clocks. School bells tell us when to stop and start, as does a referee's whistle!

p. 13 *What are you usually doing at 7:00 am? And at 7:00 pm?* e.g. Waking up, getting ready for bed. Ask children to make a chart showing what times they do things each day.

p. 17 *What is your favourite time of the year? Why?* Ask children what they like about different seasons and special celebrations or holidays.

p. 21 *How have you changed since your last birthday?* Encourage children to think about new skills as well as physical changes such as growing taller, losing teeth, growing hair.

ADVISORY TEAM

Educational Consultant
Andrea Bright – Science Co-ordinator, Trafalgar Junior School, Twickenham

Literacy Consultant
Jackie Holderness – former Senior Lecturer in Primary Education, Westminster Institute, Oxford Brookes University

Series Consultants
Anne Fussell – Early Years Teacher and University Tutor, Westminster Institute, Oxford Brookes University

David Fussell – C.Chem., FRSC

CONTENTS

© Aladdin Books Ltd 2006

Designed and produced by
Aladdin Books Ltd
2/3 Fitzroy Mews
London W1T 6DF

First published in 2006
in Great Britain
by Franklin Watts
338 Euston Road
London NW1 3BH

Franklin Watts Australia
Hachette Children's Books
Level 17/207 Kent Street
Sydney NSW 2000

ISBN 978 07496 6848 8 (H'bk)
ISBN 978 07496 7029 0 (P'bk)

A catalogue record for this
book is available from the
British Library.
Dewey Classification: 529

Printed in Malaysia
All rights reserved

Editor/Designer: Jim Pipe
Series Design: Flick, Book
Design & Graphics

Thanks to:
The pupils of Darell School,
Richmond, for appearing
as models in this book.

Photocredits:
l-left, r-right, b-bottom, t-top,
c-centre, m-middle
Cover tr, tl & b, 4tl, 5br, 6tl, 8b,
10, 12tr, 13ml, 19mr, 20, 28bl,
31bc — Marc Arundale / Select
Pictures. Cover tc, 4br, 20bl, 23b,
24 both, 30tr, 31mr — Corbis. 2tl,
13br, 15b, 19tr, 21tr, 23tr, 24tl,
26bl, 27tr, 31bl — Photodisc.
2ml & 2bl, 3, 8 both, 11 both,
12b, 14, 20b, 22br, 31ml, 32 —
istockphoto.com. 5tl — Jim Pipe.
6b, 31tr — DAJ. 7tr, 15tr, 31bl
— Iconotec.com. 7b — TongRo.
8tr, 26tr, 27bl, 28ml — Ingram
Publishing. 17tr — Digital
Vision. 17bl — Brand X Pictures.
20tr — Comstock. 22t — British
Airways. 28tr — Flat Earth.

READING ABOUT

Starters

TIME

What Time Is It?

By Sally Hewitt

Aladdin/Watts
London • Sydney

There is a **time** for most of the things we do.

Time to get up.
Time for breakfast.

Time for your favourite television programme.

There is a **time** to go to school and a **time** to go to bed.

Are you always on **time** or are you sometimes late?

4

Clock

Clocks and **watches** tell you the **time**.

You can see **clocks** all around you.

There are station **clocks**, **clocks** in cars and **clocks** on mobile phones.

Watches tell you the **time** wherever you are.

Watch

It takes about a minute to take your temperature.

We tell the time in **seconds, minutes** and **hours**.

A **second** is a short amount of time. It takes about a **second** to jump up and down once.

There are 60 **seconds** in a **minute**.

There are 60 **minutes** in an **hour**. School lunch is about an **hour** long.

There are 24 **hours** in a day. You can do lots of different things when you are awake.

Time for a walk

You sleep for about 10 hours at night.

• How long do you take to brush your teeth each night?

Long ago, people used the Sun, sand and water to **measure** time.

As the Sun moves across the sky, shadows get longer and shorter.

The moving shadow on a **sundial** points to the time.

Sundial

It takes 1 hour for all the sand in this big **hourglass** to pour from top to bottom.

This water clock uses bowls made from foil. A hole in each bowl makes it sink.

The big silver bowl takes about 1 minute to sink to the bottom.

• Will the small bowl sink slower than the big silver bowl?

9

Some clocks have a **face** and **hands**.
The short hour **hand** takes 1 hour
to go from one number to the next.

The long minute **hand** takes 1 hour
to go all the way round the clock **face**.

Minute hand

Hour hand

The second **hand** goes all the way round the clock **face** in 1 minute. You can see it moving.

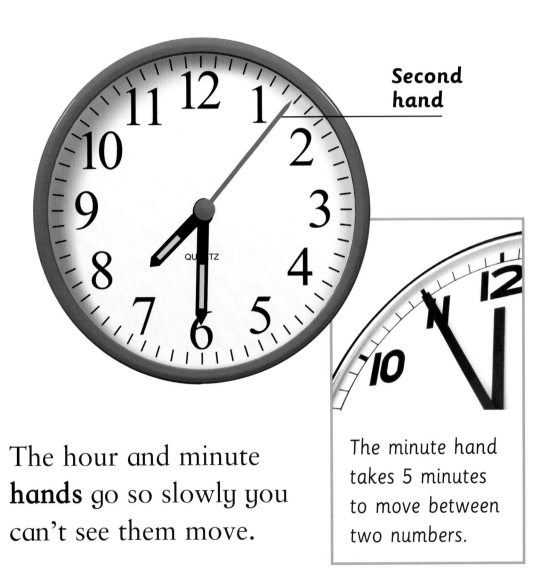

Second hand

The hour and minute **hands** go so slowly you can't see them move.

The minute hand takes 5 minutes to move between two numbers.

• What sounds tell us the time?

A **digital** clock tells the time in **numbers**.

The first two **numbers** show the hour.

The last two **numbers** show the minutes.

Digital clock

This oven has a digital clock.

The letters "am" mean **morning**.
The letters "pm" mean **afternoon**.

02:00 AM

2:00 am is
two o'clock in
the **morning**.

Asleep

02:00 PM

2:00 pm is
two o'clock in
the **afternoon**.

At school

• What are you usually doing at 7:00 am? And at 7:00 pm?

The Earth spins round in space.
It takes 24 hours, a **day** and
a **night**, to spin round once.

Earth

It is **day** time when the half of the
world you are on is facing the Sun.

It is **night** time when your half of the
world is facing away from the Sun.

There are seven **days** in a **week**. The five weekdays are Monday, Tuesday, Wednesday, Thursday and Friday.

We call Saturday and Sunday the weekend.

In term time, you go to school on weekdays.

Weekly chart

• Do you have a favourite day of the week? Why do you like it?

The Earth moves round the Sun
in a great big loop.

It takes a **year**, 365 $1/4$ days, to go
all the way round the Sun once.

**The Earth moves
round the Sun.**

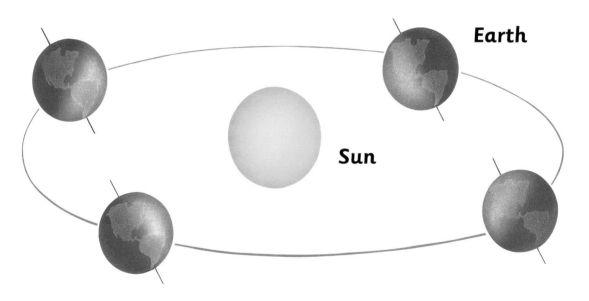

As the Earth moves round the Sun,
places get colder and warmer.
This gives us the **seasons**.

When your part of the world is nearest the Sun, it is warmer. This is summer.

When your part of the world is furthest from the Sun, it is colder. This is winter.

Summer

Winter

What is your favourite time of the year? Why?

The Moon moves round the Earth. It takes 28 days to go all the way round.

Lunar means Moon, so we call this a **lunar month**.

The Moon seems to change shape as it moves. We only see the part the Sun is shining on.

A **calendar** shows the 12 **months** of the year. There are either 30 or 31 days in most **calendar months**.

February has 28 days. Every four years, there is an extra day in the year, February 29th.

This year is called a leap year.

Calendar

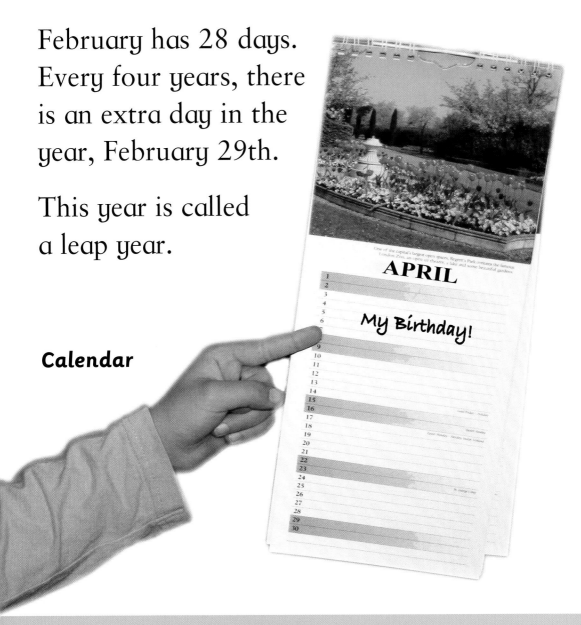

• What month is your birthday in?

You measure your **age** in years.

You start life as a baby. You **grow** into a child when you are about 2 years **old**.

You are fully **grown** when you are about 20 years **old**.

What will you look like when you are 80 years old?

Plants and animals **grow** and change too.

Tree rings

A tree makes a ring in its trunk every year. Count the rings on this tree. How **old** is it?

A baby deer **grows** quicker than you do. It is fully **grown** after about 5 years.

• How have you changed since your last birthday?

Speed is the time it takes to do something.

Plane

A plane goes **fast**. It takes about 5 hours to fly from England to America.

A ship travels **slower**. It takes about 5 days to sail from England to America.

In a race, the **fastest** person takes the least time to reach the finish. The **slowest** person takes the most time.

You can't do everything **fast!** It takes an hour to bake a cake. It takes weeks to grow a plant.

We can measure speed with a stop watch.

Race

• What do you do slowly? What do you do quickly?

MY HOLIDAY DIARY

Look out for words about **time**.

Saturday, 6.30 pm
It's the first **day** of
our **week** on holiday.
I'm sharing a room
with Josh.

We can see the sea from our window.
It's going to be the best summer
holiday ever!

I'm writing a diary to
help me remember it.

I look at the **clock**.
It's dinner **time** in half
an **hour**. I'm hungry!

24

Sunday, 7.15 pm
It's been a brilliant **day**.
We swam in the sea all
morning.

Dad took us sailing in
the **afternoon**. We're going to a firework
display later this evening.

Sunday, 10 pm
Now it's **night** and Josh is asleep already.
I can't sleep. I'm thinking about all the things
we did today. The fireworks were great!

Monday, 4 pm
Mum took us to the Fun Park.
We got there at 9:00 but it
didn't open until 10:00.

We had to wait a whole
hour! We went to a café.

I shared a big ice cream with
Josh so it wasn't too boring.

Then we had to wait
20 **minutes** in the
queue. But the rides
were fantastic!

Tuesday, 8 pm
Swimming all **day**
and no queuing!

Wednesday, 5 pm

We spent all **day**
on the beach.

Dad watched a yacht
race from the shore.

The winner was
5 **minutes faster** than
the other boats.

Josh and I had a swimming race.
I was 10 **seconds slower** than Josh,
but he was wearing flippers!

Dad **timed** us with his
digital watch.

We had a barbecue
tonight. The Moon
was very bright.

27

Thursday, 8.30 pm

Today we went to the market. I got lost!

I wanted to buy a hat. I saw a hat stall so I went and bought one.

When I looked round, I couldn't see Dad, Mum or Josh.

I looked at my **watch**. I got lost at 10:40.

I stood still.
Seconds passed.
Minutes passed.

It was 10:55 when Josh found me.
I was missing for 15 **minutes**. It felt like **ages**!

Everyone was very worried.
Mum said I shouldn't have wandered off.
Dad said I'd done the right thing,
standing still until someone found me.

Friday, 9 am
Today we are going to the water park
and I won't get lost!

Saturday, 4 pm

Home again.
It really was the
best holiday ever.

Mum took loads of
photographs. I'll stick
some in my diary.

It's a whole **year**, including winter, until our next summer holiday. 12 **months**! 365 **days**! I counted them on the **calendar**.

Look at the **clock** when you start doing something. Check it again when you finish. How long did it take?

Breakfast took me 13 minutes.

I was at school for $6\frac{1}{2}$ hours!

QUIZ

Does it take about a **second** or a **minute** to jump up and down once?

Answer on page 6

How many **hours** does it take for the Earth to spin round once?

Answer on page 14

Is the winner of a race the **fastest** or the **slowest**?

Answer on page 23

How long do these activities usually last: minutes, hours or days?

Holiday

Sleeping

Brushing teeth

Have you read this book? Well done! Do you remember these words? Look back and find out.

INDEX